the penny whistle book

By Robin Williamson

Oak Publications

New York ○ London ○ Sydney

Dedication

To Janet my Mrs. with thanks for all her help,
and with thanks to Sylvia and Tommy,
and to all who will play this music truly
and give it life, this book is dedicated.

Front and back cover photography by Janet Williamson
Book and cover design by Barbara Hoffman
Edited by Stuart Isacoff

Order No. OK 63271
US International Standard Book Number: 0.8256.0190.8
Library of Congres Card Catalog Number: 76-41141

Exclusive Distributors:
Music Sales Corporation
257 Park Avenue South, New York, NY 10010 USA
Music Sales Limited
8/9 Frith Street, London W1V 5TZ England
Music Sales Pty. Limited
120 Rothschild Street, Rosebery, Sydney, NSW 2018, Australia

Printed in the United States of America by
Vicks Lithograph and Printing Corporation

Contents

About This Book

You don't have to be a genius to play the penny whistle. If you can hum, tra-la, or tap your foot to a tune, you'll manage this book. You don't have to read music in order to commence. You'll be learning enough to play the given tunes as you go through the book step by step.

A great deal of traditional music, particularly the music of England, Scotland, and Ireland is tailor-made for the penny whistle, and all the material I've chosen here is from Britain and America. I've used well known pieces to illustrate various points of technique and throughout the book I have selected and graded from easy to more advanced some of the nicest whistle tunes I know, with a systematic approach to fingering and attention to the ancient modes.

The book is laid out in such a way as to gradually develop the necessary dexterity to play fast dance tunes and, more importantly, to develop the skill to render a tune expressively. You have to be willing to project something of yourself when you play. The tunes reveal their full emotion and meaning when they are loved, lived with, and used in life.

When I was twenty, I was living in a part of Edinburgh called "The Dumbie-dykes." One rare sunny morning a little man came down the street wearing an army coat down to his feet. He was playing the penny whistle. Housewives were leaning from high old windows and throwing pennies down to him. He was playing a tune called "The Ashgrove." Every school kid in Britain used to have this tune forced down his throat. It's a cliché, but this little man was playing it like it meant something and it did.

Truth to tell, penny whistle is one of the simplest of all instruments but in the hands of an experienced player it can make just the finest music. It's an ideal instrument for beginners but I suggest that anyone interested in fiddle playing or traditional singing would do well to get a grasp of the penny whistle, and particularly the whistler's approach to musical ornaments.

Most music stores carry two makes of whistle: the *Clarke's* in the key of C and the *Generation* in various keys. The whistle for which I've written this book is the Generation in the key of D. I decided to use this type of whistle because it is in a key which will be found very suitable when playing with other instruments such as fiddle and mandolin. I've included guitar chords as accompaniment to the tunes in this book.

Playing traditional music with your friends is a grand way to spend an evening. Anyway it beats the hell out of TV. In the old days in Scotland 80% of the population could play some instrument or sing. Now after all the "folk-reviving" of the 50's and 60's there are millions of people into folk music as a living heritage to be played, enjoyed, passed around, and to be handed down. It's an acorn that will grow another forest yet.

Background On The Whistle

Whistles of various types are found all over our planet, and people have been playing instruments very similar to the present penny whistle since the early days of the world. The first whistles were used in magic, either imitatively through the power of birdsong, or symbolically, because of their shape, in fertility rites. The Cheyenne Indians believed that certain specially potent whistles had infallible charms over women and it was forbidden by the Medieval Church in Europe to serenade with a whistle because it would be irresistible for women to hear that music by night.

In Britain, an Iron Age whistle made of sheep bone was unearthed from a burial mound in West Yorkshire and a couple of other bone whistles dating from the 12th century were excavated from High Street in Dublin.

Apart from bone, whistles have also been commonly made of clay, bamboo, and reed. Indeed any natural hollow tube has been used to make whistles at some time or other.

The word *whistle*, related to Old Scandinavian words meaning hiss and whisper, derives directly from the Old English *hwistle* meaning the act of whistling or, more basically, the throat. This basic meaning survives in the phrase "to wet your whistle." The word has a curious connection with Old English "wuduhwistle" meaning the hemlock plant from whose hollow stems whistles could have been cut.

The ancient Irish had an instrument called the *cuisle* but it was probably a reed instrument, something like a simple oboe. Their word for a whistle was *feadan* (modern Gaelic *feadog*) and *feadanaigh*, or whistle players, are mentioned in the earliest Irish laws as being amongst those who played at fairs, games, and gatherings.

The Generation whistle is usually now described as a flageolet—not really a correct description. Flageolets (a diminutive of the Old French *flageol* meaning a wind instrument) became popular in the 17th century. They had four finger holes in front and two thumb holes in back.

Many fine antique flageolets made of boxwood and ivory can be seen in museums, but the humble penny whistle, the grandfather of both the flageolet and the well known recorder, has proved immune to changing fashions. It's as perennial as the grass, and the growing interest in traditional British music ensures us a good crop of whistlers in the future.

Although it now costs more than a penny, it is still an extremely inexpensive instrument. It fits in a pocket, requires practically no special care, and is indestructible unless you run it over with a train.

Basics Part One

The Generation D whistle consists of a cylindrical metal tube pierced with six finger holes, and has a plastic mouth piece at one end. Air blown through the tip of the mouth piece is directed against a sharp edge cut into the belly of the mouthpiece. This device is called a fipple. The breaking of the air against the sharp edge causes the column of air inside the tube to vibrate.

All musical sounds are vibrations perceived through the air by the ear; slow vibrations sound low, faster vibrations sound higher. The degree of highness or lowness of a sound is called its pitch.

The whistle is sounded as follows: Place the tip of the mouthpiece between your open lips (it can be rested against the upper teeth or the teeth can be closed lightly upon it, but in this case any temptation to chew it should be resisted), and gracefully close the lips around it just firmly enough to prevent any air from escaping. Place the index, middle, and third fingers of the left hand to cover the top three holes as shown.

Notice that the pad of the end joint rather than the tip of the finger is used to cover the hole. Also take note of the position of the thumb. Blow (or rather breathe) out gently and evenly to get a soft, clear, lowish tone. The note you are playing is low G. Make sure your fingers are covering the holes completely, otherwise air will escape and the G won't sound right. If you blow too hard you won't get the low G, but higher pitched sounds instead.

Just as language can be represented by writing, so can musical sounds be represented by symbols called notes. Notes are named after the first seven letters of the alphabet: A, B, C, D, E, F, and G. These appear on a figure of five horizontal lines called a staff or stave. It looks like this:

The pitch of a note is shown by its location on the staff. At the beginning of all the pieces of music you will be playing on the whistle you will find this sign:

It is called the treble clef. It curls around the line where low G is located (this G is the G above middle C on a piano). The note low G which we just played looks like this:

The treble clef is used when writing music for instruments that sound fairly high such as the fiddle, flute, mandolin, and of course the whistle.

Now keeping the top three holes covered, place the index, middle, and third fingers of the right hand on the three lower holes. Again make sure the fingers are covering all the holes; you don't have to grip hard, just position the fingers. The left thumb goes on the underside of the whistle below the left index finger. The fingers should not be curved but flat as in the picture.

Blow or breathe out very gently and evenly to get a clear low sound. This is the lowest sound you can get on the whistle. It is the note low D. On the staff it looks like this:

Basic Fingering Chart

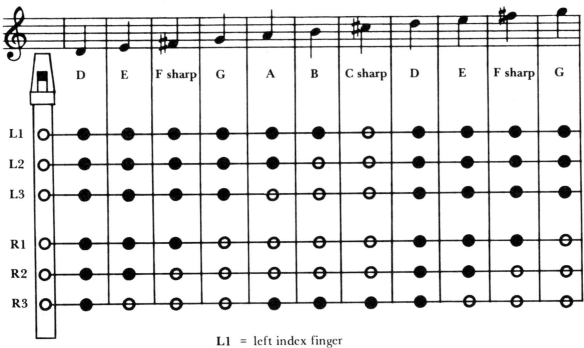

	D	E	F sharp	G	A	B	C sharp	D	E	F sharp	G

L1 = left index finger

L2 = left second finger, etc.

R1 = right index finger, etc.

black dots = holes closed

white dots = holes open

Observe that in fingering the notes A, B, and C sharp, R3 is replaced to help balance the whistle. It can be called the balance finger. As you come up from low D playing the notes in order up to C sharp, you will notice that you have to blow a little less gently as the notes rise in pitch. Above C sharp one commences a new range of notes by replacing all the fingers and blowing a little harder to obtain octave D. This is eight notes higher than low D (an octave is the interval between eight notes). Play the notes from low D up to octave D and down again in order. You are now playing the scale of D major in one octave. In the scale of D major the note F is raised in pitch half way between natural F and natural G, to F sharp; and the note C is raised in pitch halfway between natural C and natural D, to C sharp. Your whistle is set in the scale of D major, so the F and the C are already sharp as you play them using the fingering you have just learned. The symbol for a sharp, ♯, is put at the beginning of a piece of music to indicate the note or notes to be played sharp throughout that piece. So when playing pieces using the fingering just learned the sharp signs will occur at the beginning of a piece as shown:

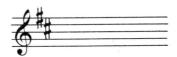

Use these notes in this exercise. A double bar line indicates the end of a piece.

Music usually has a recognizable pulse or recurrent pattern of beats. In order to represent this, written music is divided into measures of time by lines, called bars. The type of note we have used so far is called a quarter note. $\frac{3}{4}$ written at the beginning of a piece means that there are three quarter notes in each measure. Each one is to be counted as a regular and even beat. Play the following exercise counting to yourself or tapping your foot.

To produce a clean start to a note one uses the tongue. First, place the tongue against the roof of the mouth in back of the upper front teeth; then lower the tongue as you sound the note (as if to say "tuh"). To end a note cleanly put the tongue back on the roof of the mouth so that it blocks the flow of air again. Try the previous exercise again, this time using the tongue.

Octave A and octave B are fingered as they are in the low range but blown harder. To be written on the staff they require an additional small line drawn above the top of the staff called a ledger line. Here's what they look like:

Now use these notes in the following exercise. Lift the fingers cleanly when coming up, hold the lifted fingers poised in readiness over their respective whistle holes, and snap them on again cleanly when coming down.

Next comes an exercise in 4/4; four quarter notes in every measure. Count each one as an even beat; count to yourself or tap your foot while doing this exercise.

Important

1   Do not go past this stage of the book till you can produce the given notes clearly and comfortably and have a good beginning feel for the relationship between the written note and the sound you are playing.

2   If the mouthpiece gets clogged with spit the low notes won't sound properly. Put the whole mouthpiece in your mouth and blow through it vigorously. Do not point the whistle at a friend while doing this. The idea is to avoid this situation by swallowing as necessary and sounding the whistle sort of dryly.

3   If you are convinced that your breathing is even, and that your fingers are covering the holes properly, yet you still find the low note very hard to sound or the octave D difficult to get, you *may* have a faulty whistle. Take a trip down to your local music store and try out a few other Generation D whistles and see if you find a better one.

Basics Part Two

So far we have only used quarter notes, but there are other types of notes used to represent the various durations of time the note is to be continued. A whole note lasts as long as four quarter notes. This exercise uses a whole note. The double bar with the dots at the end means repeat the whole exercise from the beginning.

A half note lasts as long as two quarter notes. The following exercise uses half notes, quarter notes and a whole note.

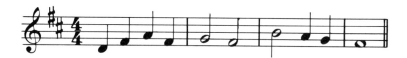

An eighth note lasts only half as long as a quarter note so you would have eight eighth notes in one measure of 4/4, counting one beat for every two eighth notes. Often you find eighth notes joined together in pairs ♪♪ which have the value of one quarter note; or in bundles of four ♫♫ which have the value of two quarter notes. Here's an exercise using eighth notes. Play it slowly measure by measure till you get the fingering fluid, then play it again getting the timing right. It's the first phrase of "Baa Baa Black Sheep."

Since the human requires air in order to continue with life, it is necessary to pause for breath when playing the whistle. But remember, music has a definite pulse, so you can't just stop anywhere or you lose the rhythm of the piece. The sign for taking a breath is ⸳. It is written above the point in the measure where the breath is to be taken. In order to get the breath in and still keep up the count of the piece it is necessary to slightly shorten the duration of the note immediately prior, though for the sake of simplicity I have not written the note as shortened.

Take a breath through the mouth; just a little air will do, as not much wind is required to play the whistle. All you have to do is take a breath regularly as marked and breathe out through the whistle while playing. If you take in too much air you may have to let some out through the nose while playing. Ideally, the breath should be taken in neatly without much of a gasp; you don't want to sound like a surfacing walrus.

Breathe where marked in the following exercises. The first is the incredibly well known tune "Yankee Doodle." Nearly every European nation claims to have originated this tune but in fact it was used as the tune to an English song which satirized

Oliver Cromwell during the early 17th century. It was later used by a British surgeon to satirize the motley armed forces he saw in young America. Finally it was taken up by the Americans themselves. When playing it, tongue all notes.

The following exercise is an octave exercise. First play it tonguing all the notes, then play it over with no tonguing. This will develop control over the use of octaves on the whistle.

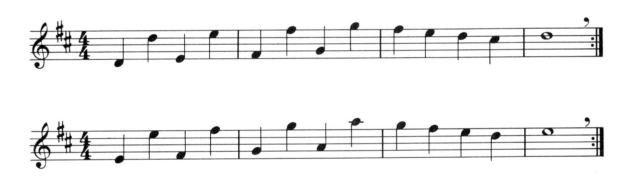

This is a good place to mention that the numbers at the beginning of a piece of music (the time signature) do not have anything to do with the speed at which the music is to be played. Some indication must be given, such as play it slowly, play it fast, etc. Go over the next exercise, "Skip to My Lou," slowly, measure by measure, getting the fingering and the timing down. If you know the tune, notice how the notes represent the melody and read it as it's written here. When you have it down, try playing it at moderate speed, tonguing all the quarter and half notes but only the first of a group of eighth notes. Stay with this tune till you can play it cleanly.

12

Play over the following exercise slowly, getting the fingering down and the timing right. When you've done this, play it at moderate speed, breathing only where indicated and tonguing only where notes are repeated.

Use a similar approach in the next exercise, but tongue only the notes in the fifth measure.

It is important to know that in approaching a piece you should first play it over measure by measure slowly, concentrating on the fingering and timing, and getting a feel for how the tune goes. Work at this till you don't have to think about where to put your fingers or what the melody is like. Then play it over at something like the indicated speed, breathing in the right places. Work at your own pace. Take enough time to get it right. Work at each tune till you feel you have improved your playing of it to the point where you feel good about it. Conviction comes naturally at that point and you can then add suitable emotion to enhance the delivery of the tune.

A Bit About Traditional Music

These tunes have a long, colourful, violent, and tangled history, and it's often hard to say where or how they originated. In general it is true that a traditional tune, as it comes down to us, is not the work of a single composer so much as the work of the many musicians through whose hearts and hands the tune has passed. As tunes percolate through lifetimes they are embroidered upon; new variations are added, the title of a tune may change, or a player who popularizes a tune in his area may lend his name to it.

16th, 17th, and 18th century musicians and poets frequently wrote new songs to old tunes or sometimes annexed tunes and credited themselves with the authorship. Early English printed music is more plentiful than early Scots or Irish printed music and it is thickly peppered with provenly Scots and Irish tunes. Many Irish reels and airs can be traced to Scots originals, and many Scots jigs and airs can be traced to Irish originals. But obviously all three countries produced brilliant music of their own. Between Ireland and Scotland there is an affinity of blood and there has always been a great deal of interchange between the two countries. One whole branch of my family comes from Ireland, another from the Highlands, and a third from the Lowlands of Scotland.

It's a mistake of certain Irish authors over the last hundred years to bend over backwards trying to prove as many tunes as possible to be of Irish origin. Even the O'Neills in their monumental musical research have a tendency to flavour the truth with a dash of Irish ketchup.

Broadly speaking, English music tends to have an elegance and prettiness in its simplicity or courtliness. Irish music tends to be nimble, elaborate, and graphic and more melodic than chordal. Scots music tends to be craggy, jocund, and haunting, more chordal than Irish music and often a bit slower.

Tunes

THE ASHGROVE

The tune to this very well known song is from Wales. Work at getting the flow of breath to each note even and controlled; this is the way to develop a sweet and singing tone. Tongue all the quarter and half notes but only the first of any group of eighth notes. The tune goes moderately slow and smooth as a smooth river.

THE DRUNKEN SAILOR

Play a low E. Now play all the notes in order from that E up to the octave E. You are now playing all the notes found in the scale of D major but starting from a foundation of E (second degree of the scale) instead of the D. A range of notes like this based on the second degree of a major scale is called a Dorian mode.

"The Drunken Sailor" is an easy example of a Dorian mode melody. Perhaps the best known of all sea songs, it is a capstan chanty to be sung when hauling up the anchor of an old sailing ship.

In order to tongue pairs of eighth notes, make the tongue shapes TUH and KUH. The tonguing of the first two measures here goes TAH TUH KUH TAH TUH KUH, TAH TAH TAH TAH.

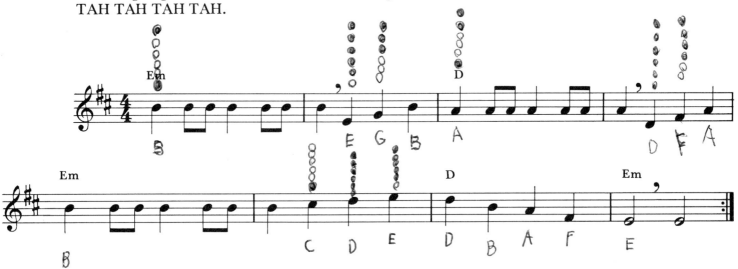

RAMBLE AWAY

This is another tune in the Dorian mode, a song tune from the Midlands of England. Play it gently, tonguing only the first note of each measure except where the same note is to be repeated, or after a breath. The emotion of the tune is a wistful remembrance of bygone escapades.

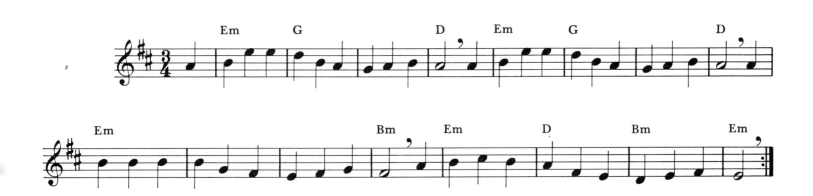

LOVELY JOAN

This tune, again in the Dorian mode, is from the South of England. You will observe that various quarter notes have a dot after them and are followed by eighth notes. A dot after a note indicates that it is to be played half as long again as its original value. The note after it is thus halved in value. Basically the effect of a dot after a note is to give emphasis to that note.

In this tune try tonguing the first and third beats of each measure, except where the same note is to be repeated.

This is a really pretty tune with a misty feel of eternal romance.

SHADY GROVE

Play all the notes in order from B up to octave B. A range of notes based like this on the sixth degree of a major scale is called an Aeolian mode. The well known American tune "Shady Grove" is a good example of a melody in the Aeolian mode. Try tonguing all notes but only the first of any group of eighth notes.

SEARCHING FOR LAMBS

You will have gathered by now that tonguing is an effect which can be used in various ways to help pronounce a tune. From here on through the book I suggest you use tonguing where it seems suitable to you.

When playing the third and fourth measures here you will find it more convenient to use R2 to balance the whistle rather than R3. Changes between octave E and the C sharp below it are thus easily managed.

This fine tune in the Aeolian mode is from Southern England. A beautiful girl met by midsummer dawn in meads of tangled grasses. Her bare feet and the hem of her skirt are wet with dew. Sun flares through mist that hovers in the low ground. "Searching for Lambs."

FAREWELL AND ADIEU YE FINE SPANISH LADIES

When I was about six my grandmother took me to visit the town of Canterbury. It was a blustery April afternoon that we left outside, to pace in the stillness of the Cathedral.

Later, while looking for a tea shop we passed by a shop that sold musical instruments, and I, being mad crazy about musical instruments, persuaded her to buy me a penny whistle. That was the first one I ever had.

It wasn't long after that I heard someone singing this song on the radio, but it was a while before I figured how to set it on the whistle so as to get all the notes in.

It's an English tune, probably from the 17th century, again in the Aeolian mode; it goes dreamily and regretfully.

This is an exercise which helps the fingers get used to working in various patterns. Play it over slowly, measure by measure, and when fluent play it right through breathing as indicated. Lift the fingers cleanly and snap 'em on again crisply.

SOLDIER'S JOY

"Soldier's Joy" has to be about the most wide spread of all fiddle tunes. This is a simple setting of it in D major. There are two parts, each to be repeated. Use R2 as the balance finger for the second to last measure in each part.

Always use R2 as the balance finger when moving from octave E to the C sharp below. Otherwise use R3 as usual.

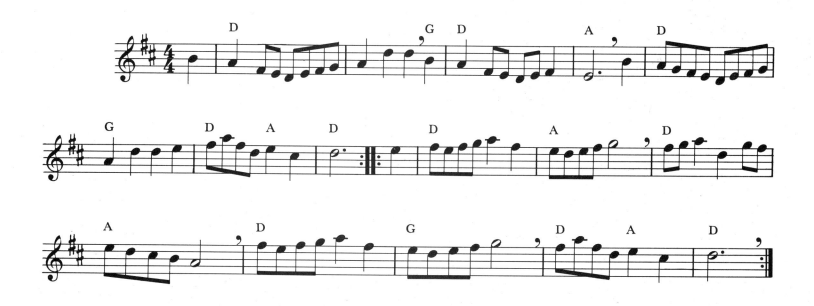

THE ROSE TREE

This tune used to be known in Ireland as "Moirin ni Chuileannain" or "Little Mary Cullinan," a title derived from the song written to this tune by the Irish poet John O'Tuomy, who died in 1775. In his song the girl's name was an allegory of Ireland.

The tune was first published in Scotland in Thompson's *Country Dances*, 1774, there called "The Irish Lilt." It was reprinted again in Scotland in Oswald's *Caledonian Pocket Companion*, 1760, titled "The Gimlet," and again in Gow's *Second Collection*, 1788, there titled "The Old Lea Rigg" or "The Rose Tree."

The tune is extremely well known in England as a Morris dance tune and the simple setting here is pretty much the way it's played in England. It goes brightly and proudly but not too fast.

THE TOUCHSTONE

A touchstone is a stone used to test the purity of gold and hence has come to mean any standard of excellence or quality. The tune here is an 18th century English country dance tune which is not at all tarnished. It goes cheerfully, not too fast.

SHEPHERD'S HEY

The word *hey* or *hay* was used to describe an English dance as long ago as the 16th century. Nowadays "The Hey" is a figure in country dancing where lines of dancers weave through and through. This extremely well known tune goes perfectly happily, not too fast.

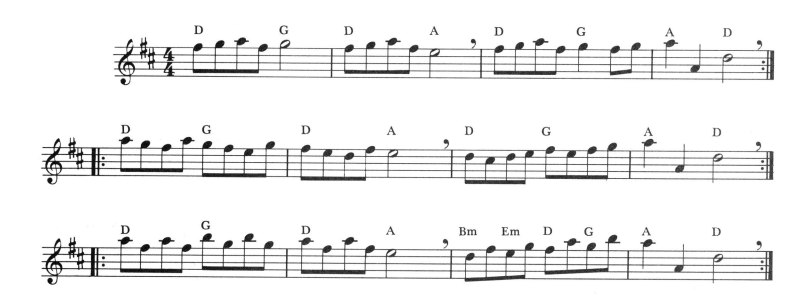

THE LASS OF RICHMOND HILL

Play the note octave F sharp. Now rapidly bounce that index finger up and down. That's a trill on F sharp. Now trill octave E and B in the same way. A trill is marked tr above the written note. These three trills occur in this tune.

The words to this tune were written by barrister Leonard McNally to a girl in Yorkshire who became his wife in 1787. The tune was written by one James Hook and the song was first performed on stage at Vauxhall Gardens, London, in the year of McNally's marriage. Play it gently with smooth sounding notes.

HEWLETT

This Irish tune is traditionally attributed to the most famous of all Irish harpers, Carolan (1670-1738). It's a good tune of the type known as a *planxty*, usually a tune made in honor of a patron and not necessarily bound to the even structure of dance music.

Trills occur here on A and G. In playing the first part of the tune the first time through, end with the measure marked 1; when you repeat the first part, end with the measure marked 2.

The tune is cocky and full of well being. Don't play it too fast.

STAR OF THE COUNTY DOWN

Though so far the only melodic decoration we have looked at is the trill, there are quite a few traditional musical ornaments—various twiddles of the fingers that can be used to decorate a tune.

In this tune two ornaments occur: the triplet and the smear. The triplet (three linked eighth notes marked with a 3) is to be played in the time that would normally be occupied by two eighth notes or one quarter note.

A smear (marked sm above the written note) is to be played by fingering the note below the written note and gradually smearing the finger across the finger hole towards the hand so that the sound slides up to the pitch as written. To smear the note octave E, for example, one fingers octave D and gradually removes R3. Practice smearing various notes until you can do it with ease.

The tune here is very well known, played all over Ireland, and was probably written in Southwest Ireland by some unknown musician in the 18th century. In Britain, America and Canada it's known as "When a Man's in Love." It goes along boldly, like a march.

JOHNNIE FAA

Tiny notes like this: ♪ are called single grace notes. They are little ornamental notes which are hinted at before the note that follows them. They occupy no time in the measure, theoretically. If a grace note C sharp occurs before a B as in the last measure of the first part of this tune, one plays the C sharp for an instant before snapping on L1 to finger the B. That's all there is to it.

Faa was the traditional family name of kings of the Gypsies. Calling themselves the Lords of Little Egypt, they had rights of free passage through all the lands of Scotland, as confirmed by the King of Scots during the 15th century.

This tune is traditionally associated with the oldest versions of a song cycle in which a handsome gypsy charms away a rich man's wife. The songs evolved from the cuckolding of a Scots nobleman named Lord Cassilis, upon whose lovely lady the gypsies cast their *glamour*.

Glamour is the gypsy power to exert fascination and hypnotically or otherwise create illusions. Once upon a time at Haddington in the Borders of Scotland a gypsy was making a fortune in the streets exhibiting a farmyard cock who could pull an oak tree along with its beak. All was going well for the gypsy till an old man came by with a cart full of clover. There must have been a four leafed clover somewhere in his bundle, because suddenly everyone could see plainly that the cock was tugging merely at a straw. It was then that the gypsy had to flee for his life. So now you know, four leafed clovers dispell illusion.

The tune here was first printed in *Most Favourite Scots Songs*, London 1790. It probably pre-dates that by a long-shot. Play the tune firmly and sadly.

THE CHANTER'S SONG

Play all the notes in order between A and octave A. A range of notes like this beginning on the fifth degree of a scale is called the Mixolydian mode. The tune here is an Irish march in the Mixolydian mode. The chanter of a set of bagpipes is where the finger holes are and where the tune comes out. A similar melody to this one occurs in versions of the English song "The Rambling Sailor." "The Chanter's Song" also has single grace notes. It goes firmly, at a good walking pace.

THE DAWNING OF THE DAY

One new feature here is the dotted and halved eighth notes in the sixth measure. The dotted eighth note becomes half as long again as a regular eighth note. The note that follows it is halved by the addition of an extra tail to become a sixteenth note. The sixth measure thus sounds something like: DAH DIH DUM DUM DAH DIH.

Another new feature here is the double grace note. It's the same idea as the single grace note, you just hint at the two little notes before the note that follows them.

The tune is another Irish one in the Mixolydian mode. Its authorship is attributed to Thomas Connelan, the harper, born at Cloonmahon, County Sligo, around 1640. His name for the tune was "The Golden Star," perhaps that star which shines bright and lonely in the dark before the dawn. Watch it from a moor sometime, or the top of a hill, to get the feel of the tune. The setting here is based on a bagpipe slow march version.

HOLLAND'S A FINE PLACE

The sign ∾ indicates the type of ornament known as a turn. It occurs here in the fifth measure. Play the written note, then very briskly play the note above, the written note again, the note below, and the written note again.

The accent is on the first note, the rest is just a flick of the fingers. To get the timing right, first play the measure without the ornament, then add it so that the entire figure occupies the same time as the note it's written over.

The Irish tune here is another slow march in the Mixolydian mode. The sadness of it belies its title, which may relate to the loyalists who followed the exiled Stuart heir to Holland after Oliver Cromwell's coup d'etat of 1649. Or maybe it's one of the possible tunes to the Scots ballad "The Lowlands of Holland."

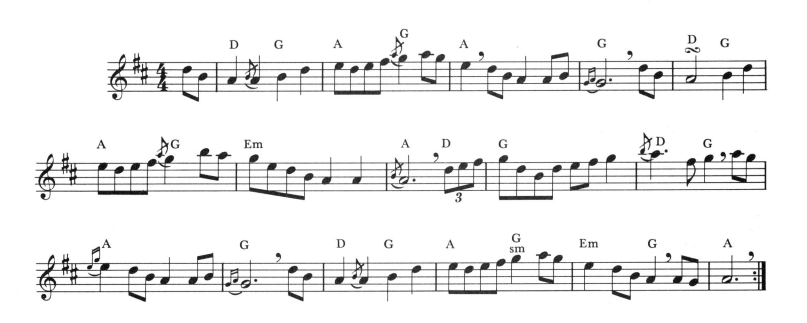

GILLIEKRANKIE

The name of this tune commemorates a battle fought at the pass now called Killiecrankie above Blair Athol in Perthshire, Scotland, on the 27th of July, 1689. Highland clans entirely routed a Dutch-English army commanded by one General Mackay. The Highland leader, James Claverhouse, known as Bonnie Dundee, was killed in the battle.

Carolan wrote a song to this tune and the tune is known in Ireland today as "Planxty Davis" but the tune was current in Scotland shortly after the date of the battle, before Carolan's birth. It's possible that this tune was written by Thomas Connelan. Connelan spent most of his adult life in Scotland and according to Bunting, the Irish collector, and Arthur O'Neill, the 18th century harper, he became a dignitary of Edinburgh and, at length, died in that fair city. Gratton Flood, the Irish musical historian, would have it that he returned to Ireland in 1689, died there in 1698 at Bouchier Castle near Lough Gur, County Limerick, and was buried at Temple Nuadh nearby while a banshee howled lugubriously.

Whatever, this is a valiant and cocky tune and goes at a good marching pace.

RAKES OF MALLOW

This tune features the note high D.

This is the highest note easily obtainable on the whistle. You have to tongue and blow sharply to sound it. Play the notes octave A, octave B, octave C sharp (same fingering as low C sharp), and high D up and down a few times before you try the tune over.

Mallow is a town on the river Blackwater in County Cork. It was famous during the 18th century as a spa resort, and a contemporary song described the rakes in their revels there as "Beauing, belleing, dancing, drinking," and generally cutting loose.

The tune was first printed in Burk Thumoth's *Twelve English and Twelve Irish Airs*, 1745. In 1751 it was reprinted in Johnson's *Two Hundred Country Dances*, now with a title: The Rakes of London. Later in the same publisher's *Compleat Tutor for Guitar* it was called "The Rakes of Marlow."

The tune is widely known throughout the British Isles as a country dance tune, particularly in England. It goes unashamedly brightly.

THE SKYE BOAT SONG

6/4 time is just like 3/4 or waltz time except there are two counts of three beats in each measure (1,2,3; 1,2,3). Notes joined with a tie ⌢ are to be phrased together with an unbroken flow of sound. The syllable *rit.* written below the second to last measure is short for *ritardando* and means slow down as you play the last two measures.

This tune was originally used as a rowing tune in the Western Isles of Scotland. It was only in the last hundred years that the famous speed-bonny-boat words were added.

The Isle of Skye is bounteously endowed with legend. Famous among the island's clan chiefs are the MacLeods of Dunvegan, who treasure as an heirloom a fairy flag, the *Bratach Sith*. This was traditionally given to a 14th century MacLeod by his fairy wife as a farewell gift when she would return to Fairyland after twenty years of marriage. The place of their parting is still known as the *Fairy Bridge*.

A "rational" explanation of the flag observes that the Norse king, Harold Hardrada, from whom the MacLeods trace descent, set out upon an ill-fated expedition to England in 1066, taking with him a magic flag named *Land-Ravager*. Maybe this was the Bratach Sith.

An expert who examined the flag not so long ago reckoned the cloth had similarities to early Syrian textiles, and there is another tale about the flag which states that a MacLeod was given it during the Crusades by a water sprite.

SHEEBEG SHEEMORE

This tune, originally known as "The Bonny Cuckoo," was used by Carolan as the melody for his first song. A certain Squire Reynolds of Lough Scur, County Leitrim, suggested Carolan should try his hand at songwriting and ventured as a theme the hostilities betwixt two local Fairy Courts, one on the hill Sheebeg (the Little Fairy Hill) and the other on Sheemore (the Big Fairy Hill). The bones of the legendary hero Fionn Mac Cumhail (Finn McCool) are believed to be buried under a mound on Sheebeg.

This is a lovely liquid tune that flows as strong as whiskey and falls as sad as rain. Play it boldly at a moderate speed.

GOD REST YE MERRY, GENTLEMEN

A traditional London carol in the Aeolian mode, this well known melody is the best example I can think of to introduce 6/8 or jig time. Two groups of three eighth notes in each measure give it a light, fast 1,2,3; 1,2,3. The prevalant note pattern here of quarter notes and eighth notes sounds something like <u>DUM</u> dih <u>DUM</u> dih in each measure. This type of note pattern in 6/8 is called a *single jig*.

SCOTCH CAP

Scots music seems to have exercised a strong fascination in English fashionable circles from the 16th century up to the 19th century. Many Scots tunes were printed in Playford's *English Dancing Master* during the 17th century. This single jig was printed by Playford.

It's an interesting tune in the Dorian mode, and goes at a moderate tempo. The cap in the title may well refer to a nightcap or last drink before going to bed.

CUCKOLD'S ALL AWRY

Samuel Pepys makes mention of this dance in his famous 17th century diaries.
"Then to country dances; the King leading the first which he called for; which was, says he, 'Cuckold's All Awry,' the old dance of England. Of all the ladies that danced, the Duke of Monmouth's mistress and my Lady of Castlemaine, and a daughter of Sir Harry de Vicke's were the best. The manner was when the king dances all the ladies in the room, and the Queen herself, stand up; and indeed he dances rarely, and much better than the Duke of York. Having stayed there as long as I thought fit, to my infinite content, it being the greatest pleasure I could wish now to see at court, I went home, leaving them dancing."

Notice that in the second half of the third measure in the second part of the tune the eighth note comes before the quarter note; that measure sounds something like DUM dih dih DUM. The tune goes elegantly, at a moderate speed.

Repeat from beginning

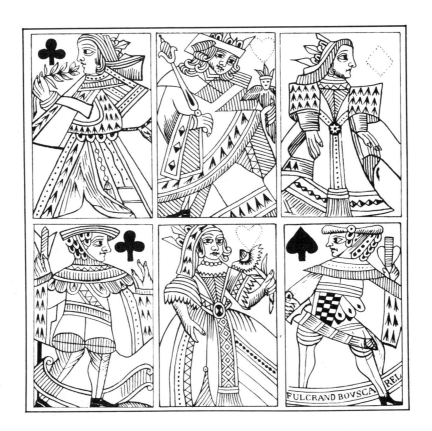

34

This is a new fingering for octave D. All fingers on, except L1.

Now by lifting off R2 you get the note C natural.

This fingering of C natural can be called *forked fingering*. Use these fingerings to play the following exercise. Notice that the key signature has only F sharp marked now. The C is natural.

SWEET BETSY FROM PIKE

Using the fingering just learned, play over this well known song tune. It's a good introduction to the key of G major: all the notes between G and octave G with the C natural.

In Ireland this tune is used for a song called "The Old Orange Flute," and for another about a sporting greyhound called "Master McGrath" (pronounced Mc-Graw).

I SAW THREE SHIPS

Try the same fingering on this well known carol: a single jig in G major. It's an English tune.

TWO BROTHERS

Play all the notes between A and octave A keeping the C natural. You are now playing a Dorian mode built on the second degree of the G scale.

"Two Brothers" is an American tune in this mode; it relates to the Civil War. It goes quite slowly.

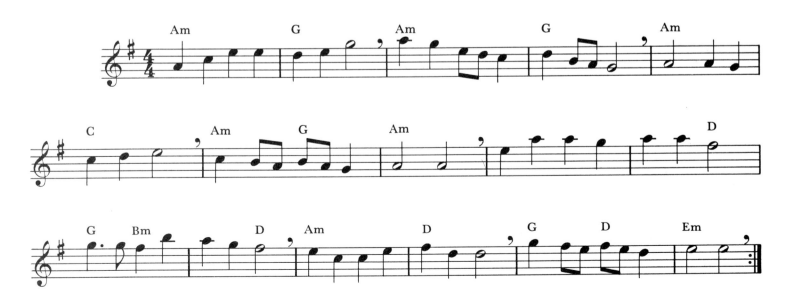

THE SHAN VAN VOCHT

The grace notes in this tune are single grace notes of the type sometimes known as *cuts*. Finger, but do not sound, the note which is to follow the cut. Then momentarily lift and replace the appropriate finger to make the cut, without removing any other fingers. This technique, called *cutting*, derives from the bagpipe. I have marked in L1 and L2 to indicate which fingers to cut with.

The D grace note at the beginning of the second part is performed by momentarily fingering octave D in the recently learned way and then removing R2.

The title of the tune here is a phonetic spelling of the original Gaelic which means *the poor old woman*: a symbol of Ireland. The tune is known in Scotland as "The Thorn Bush in Oor Kail Yaird." I have included phrases of the Scots tune in this version. Play hesitantly and regretfully.

There is another way of fingering C natural which is particularly useful when moving from a C to notes below it. It is done by putting L1 on as if to finger B, but keeping the tip of the finger rolled back towards the left, half-uncovering the top hole. This gives you a serviceable C natural and you can then roll the tip of the finger on to cover the hole to get the B. This technique is called *half covering*. Try it in this exercise.

THE LASS OF PATIE'S MILL

The C's are half covered throughout this piece. It's an old Scots tune for which words, highly praised by Robert Burns, were written by the poet Alan Ramsay and published in his *Tea Table Miscellany*, 1724. The tune was first printed in Thomson's *Orpheus Caledonius*, 1725.

The Irish collector Bunting, in his *Second Collection of Ancient Music of Ireland*, 1809, prints a tune he calls "Carolan's Cap" which appears to be an elaboration of the tune here.

Play it swaggeringly with a bounce.

AN GIOLLA RUADH

Pronounced *an geely rooach*, this Irish tune is also well known in America by its English title "The Red Haired Boy." It's the tune for the song "The Little Beggarman." It's also sometimes called "Gilderoy," which is a corruption of the Gaelic title.

We're back in the Mixolydian mode here, with two sharps in the key signature. The triplet of A's in the first part, seventh measure, has to be tongued. Try making the tongue shapes TUH KUH TUH.

The tune should go jauntily, medium fast. It's a type of dance tune called a *hornpipe*.

Here is an exercise which employs a third useful fingering for C natural, to be used when moving from octave E to a C below.

This fingering uses R2 as balance finger and it occurs in the third and fourth measures of this exercise.

TWA BONNIE MAIDENS

A Scots hornpipe, sometimes called "Prince Charles' Welcome to the Isle of Skye." The title refers to the time after the quelling of the 1745 Rebellion when Charles Stuart fled to Skye disguised as Betty Burke, an Irish servant girl, in the company of Flora MacDonald.

The MacDonalds owned a fertile area of Skye known as Sleat, south of the wild Cuillin Mountains. Prince Charley was sheltered at the house of Mugstot in Kilbride near Torrin until he was able to take ship overseas. He made his way to Rome where, in the end, he died of drink.

While brutal reprisals were being carried out in the Highlands, Flora MacDonald was captured and was amazed to find herself the darling of English high society. Later she married a kinsman, Allan MacDonald, and emigrated to Carolina.

The same tune was attributed to Carolan under the title of "Planxty George Brabazon" by the Irish collector O'Neill in 1903. No one seems to know just why he did this.

The tune goes jauntily with a lilting swing.

This is another exercise to develop dexterity. Use R2 as balance finger in the fifth measure and in the seventh measure.

SOLDIER'S JOY

I adapted this more intricate version of the tune from a bagpipe setting. Play it like a hornpipe, jauntily not too fast.

THE BLACK NAG

This is an English jig in the Aeolian mode. It is the type of jig known as a *double jig* on account of the prevalent note pattern.

Take care in the fingering of the second part. Try using R1 as a balance finger. When you have the tune down it should go moderately fast.

Nag is an old word originally meaning a small saddle horse and later acquiring the meaning of any horse, particularly a crook-backed, bandy-legged, toothless bargain.

DOMNALL NA GREINE

In tonguing these groups of notes where the same note is to be repeated, try using the tongue shapes TUH KUH TUH.

Play the tune over till fluent, then add the turns. Make sure you get all the notes of the turn distinct.

The title of the tune means *Daniel of the sun*. This sunny Dan was apparently a lazy fellow, much given to basking and living by the old Highland adage, "never put off till tomorrow what you can do the following day." His exploits inspired witty creations from several 18th century Munster poets.

This is an Irish double jig; it goes fast.

THE TENPENNY BIT

Another Irish double jig, this time in the Mixolydian mode. The A cuts are to be performed with L3. Versions of this tune were collected in the early years of this century by James O'Neill from Abram Beamish of Cork and James Kennedy of County Leitrim. The tune is believed to be of some antiquity.

THE HEATHER GLEN

This is a classic, pleasant and full fledged hornpipe. When I think of heather I remember enough heathery miles to shine away two pairs of oily boots; times I've been flat on my face on heather by moorland waters after a trout; and times I've been flat on my back among the heather courting or drunk. It's among the heather I've sung and seen visions, and taken great resolves and thrown stones at adders and outrun ghosts and cried and forgotten sadness.

THE HUMOURS OF TUAIMGRÉINE

Another Irish hornpipe, this is in the Dorian mode of the G scale. The C natural trill that occurs in this tune is played by fingering the forked C natural position and bouncing R2.

Tuaimgréine is a small town in County Claire, with a ruined castle where the O'Gradeys used to lord it. The old church there was restored in the 10th century by the Irish hero-king Brian Boru. Brian was famous for his warmaking upon the Danes in Ireland. After years of strife he became, first, king of the South of Ireland, and later *Ard Ri* or high king of all Ireland. Finally, in his seventieth year, he drove the Vikings out of the country altogether at the battle of Clontarf, where he himself was killed.

But Brian's greatest achievement was to create a cultural and religious revival in Ireland. Prior to the 10th century, learning had been nourished and fostered in monasteries; but the Vikings had raised Cain over that. Brian Boru founded a new secular order, the Bardic Order, and the Bards were the intellectual movers and shakers of the land for five hundred years and inspired beyond that an enduring heritage.

A harp which traditionally is supposed to have belonged to Brian Boru can still be seen in Dublin.

THE JOB OF JOURNEYWORK

This is an Irish set dance tune; that's to say a tune which has a special dance that goes with it. The sign ♮ means that the note so marked is to be played natural within that measure. In the measures following the natural sign, however, the key signature is in effect again until another note is marked natural.

A journeyman was originally a man hired to work by the day; the word came to mean a tradesman who had served his apprenticeship and had become skilled. So journeywork would mean work done by a skilled craftsman. Judging by some of the tradesmen it's been my misfortune to employ at one time or other, journeywork is in danger of extinction and needs reviving. And damn, this tune deserves to be out on the road again. It's a great tune. It can be played either like a hornpipe or a bit slower.

O'KEEFE'S SLIDE

12/8 time has a similar feel to 6/8 but there are four groups of three eighth notes in each measure. Tunes in 12/8 are often called *slides*, sometimes pronounced *shlides* either affectionately or drunkenly. They go the same tempo as single jigs, moderately fast. This one is in the Dorian mode of the G scale but the C natural is left out entirely. When a note is consistently omitted from a mode or scale throughout a piece of music, the piece is said to be in a *gapped mode* or scale. Gapped modes are a feature of early traditional music.

MERRILY KISS THE QUAKER'S WIFE

When playing the turn in the second measure of the first part here, use C for the top note of the turn. Play the note A, then cut with L1 (momentarily lift L1 so a sort of C natural sounds, then replace it so the A sounds again), then briskly play the note G, and A again.

The C cut which follows this turn in measure two is done with L1. The triplets which occur in this tune have the value of one eighth note.

The tune here is another Irish slide, this time in G major. Slides are particularly associated with Kerry. There is a Scots tune called "The Quaker's Wife" to which the first part of the tune here bears some resemblance.

THE ROCKY ROAD TO DUBLIN

Tunes in 9/8 time are known as *slip jigs:* three groups of three eighth notes in each measure. This is a very well known tune to which the song of the same name is usually sung. The tune goes round and round in circles. Therefore, to end after several repeats play the first measure of the first part and stop, hopefully not dizzily gasping.

This is not an old tune. The earliest printed version occurs in *Citizen Magazine*, Dublin, 1841. It is described there as a modern dance tune and the name is stated to be that of a road near Clonmel. The tune became extremely popular from there on out and Irish nursemaids in those days used to frequently recommend themselves for employment by stating that they could sing, and dance the baby to "The Rocky Road." It's a miracle any of the babies survived without being disjointed entirely.

I've adapted this setting from a bagpipe version. It's in the Mixolydian mode and it goes quite fast.

It may be as well to mention that in hitching through Ireland I've observed it to be a considerably rockier road to Belfast than it is to Dublin.

Repeat from beginning

49

HARDIMAN THE FIDDLER

Another slip jig from Ireland. This one features cuts with L1 and L3 and a turn on A with C as the top note. It goes best in moderate tempo.

This is a really intriguing tune. Exactly who Hardiman was I'm not sure but he must have been good and by the time you can play this one on the whistle you can call yourself "Hardiman the Whistler."

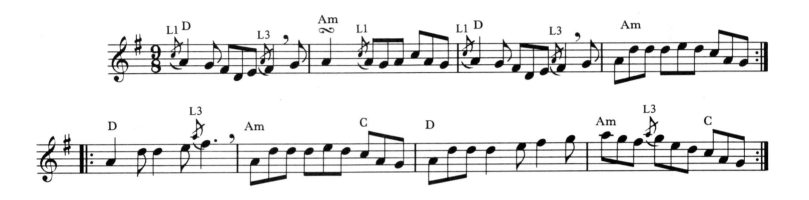

THE DUSTY MILLER

This Irish slip jig sounds good when played fast. The guitar accompaniment can play in 3/4.

When I was living in Wales I used to go to get flour and oatmeal from a miller at an old water mill away up a valley. All the wooden parts of the mill would be clacking and thudding and the grain would be shifting in the hopper and spilling between the grindstones and the water would be tumbling and the wheel turning all in different rhythms. He was a great old man and he had an old friend who in his youth had been the captain of a sailing clipper. It was a great place to take a drink as a precaution against the damp and I wish I'd written down some of the stories the old men knew. Anyway this tune would fit in perfectly.

OLD MOLLY HARE

This simple reel is known in Scotland as "The Fairy Dance" and is widely known in America by its Appalachian title, as above. Reels are always in 4/4 but played fast enough so that the foot taps comfortably two to each measure. The foot taps on the first and third beats.

Repeat from beginning

ARKANSAS TRAVELLER

This has to be about the best known of all American fiddle tunes. There was a play called *The Arkansas Traveller* which made a big splash in Ohio in 1850. It concerned a traveller who encountered an Arkansas squatter sitting in his cabin, playing away at this tune which he learned in New Orleans. The whole play revolved around the squatter's attempts to remember the end of the tune.

The G sharps in the seventh measure of both the first and second parts are to be played by half covering the G hole.

Fiddle players usually render this tune very fast. It's a pretty easy tune on the fiddle. It should go quite fast, just do it as fast as you can make it sound good on the whistle.

ABSENT MINDED WOMAN

This is an Irish reel which goes the same speed as "Old Molly Hare." Actually all the women with whom it has been my pleasure to associate have been a great deal less absent minded than me, and my mrs. is extremely unabsent minded. That said, this is a really nice tune.

The source of this tune was a certain Mrs. Carey of County Limerick whose husband, John Carey the fiddler, knew a cartload of tunes. This was one he didn't know.

OLD MAIDS OF GALWAY

This is an Irish reel in the Dorian mode. If you find your fingers starting to flick out grace notes besides the written graces, you're on the right track. Galway reels are famous for their emotive and misty qualities. This fine lonesome reel goes briskly with sadness in it.

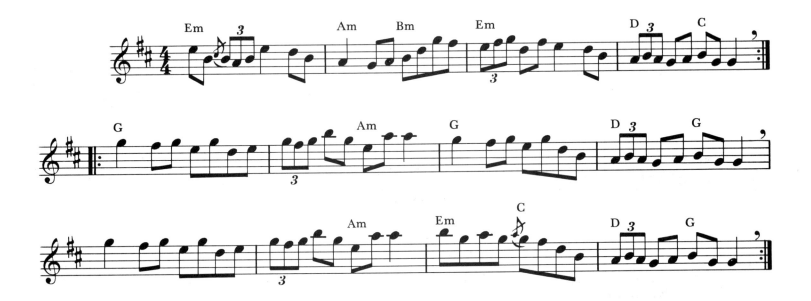

BLACKBERRY BLOSSOM

This one is a very nice American fiddle tune which shows more than a trace of its Celtic origins. It is usually played quite fast; try playing it about hornpipe speed.

By the way, blackberry blossom makes quite a nice cup of tea if you pick the flowers and dry them out. At least the Scots kind does. I imagine it's the same in America.

Repeat from beginning

THE BOATMAN OF PITNACREE

This is a Scots reel slightly slower than most. Pitnacree is a country seat in Perthshire, four miles north of Aberfeldy, by the river Tay. The boatman there would likely know all the stretches of the river like the back of his weathered hand, and where the good salmon would be lying after the gentlemen went home with their rods and reels and empty baskets. Picture him out again by the riverside, stepping softly through the darkness with his lantern and his gaff.

Repeat from beginning

LOCHABER NO MORE

Observe here that some of the dotted eighth notes occur as the second note of a pair giving the effect dih <u>DEE</u>. Also observe the usage of the turns in this tune. The F natural which occurs in the second part, measures nine and ten, is to be played by smearing back R2 so that the E hole is half covered.

Thomas Connelan claimed authorship of this tune, but harpers at the Belfast harp meeting, 1792, unanimously attributed it to a slightly earlier Irish harper, Miles O'Reilly, born 1635 at Killincarra (near Bailieborough) in the County Cavan. He called the tune "Limerick's Lamentation" or "King James' March to Ireland." The title relates to the defeat of James II by William of Orange. Actually, further research on the background of the tune by Donal O'Sullivan and others proves it to be of Highland Scottish origin. O'Reilly may well have elaborated on the tune and/or popularized it in his area.

"Lochaber No More" is still played by Highland regimental pipers as a lament but the tune here is a version originally set for the fiddle from Davie's *Caledonian Repository*, 1829.

This is a beautiful, sad air to be played slowly. As in singing, a vibrato can be produced where muscles of the diaphragm (look at an illustration in a good dictionary) pulse naturally as the lungs deflate. This effect sounds particularly pleasing on long highish notes as in this tune, but don't go tieing yourself in knots trying to achieve it. Just keep on working with well filled lungs, moving plenty of breath through the whistle; one day the effect should just occur.

JENNY DANG THE WEAVER

Regarding the title, perhaps a certain North country belle assaulted some poor weaver; but there is another possibility. The spinning jenny was the first spinning machine on which a number of threads could be spun simultaneously. It was invented about 1767 by James Hargreaves of Lancashire. The weavers would likely be hard put to match their cloth output to the supply of wool. Weavers were legendarily industrious, but in those days they had to work from dawn to dusk just to scrape by. Picture the weaver hunched at his loom, throwing the shuttle back and forth and grinning wryly to himself as he hums this tune under his breath.

A fine old Scots reel, you'll probably find it goes best a bit slower than most reels.

THE HAG WITH THE MONEY

The Welsh were, at one time, hosts to a mountain spirit called "The Hag with the Dribble." It was her custom to lament the imminent deaths of prominent persons by filling her apron full of rocks and flying through the air dropping them randomly from great heights, this being the dribble.

I don't imagine the hag, for whom this tune was named, used to throw her money around too much. Picture her huddled by a dead peat fire $crongeing her coins.

This is an intriguing tune, the first part having one sharp and the second part two sharps. The turns have C as the top note. It should go a bit slower than most jigs to get the beauty out of it. The tune was a favourite of O'Neill's friend James McFadden, the fiddler, during the early years of this century. I first heard the tune played by my friend Finbar Furey who I consider to be one of the best pipers I've ever heard.

It's a magnificent and graphic Irish slow jig, with an extraordinary mixture of pathos, wit, and genuine tragedy.

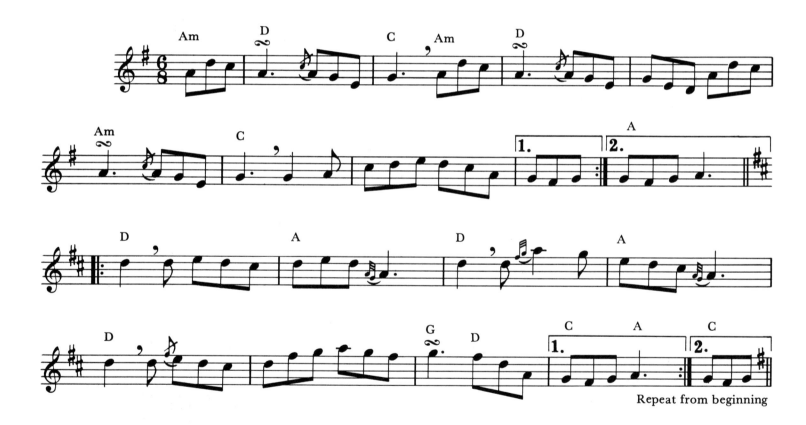

Repeat from beginning

GIVE ME YOUR HAND

This very pleasant air should be played at moderate speed. Play it all through and then repeat from the beginning, ending at the close of the eighth measure.

Rory Dall O'Cathain (Blind Roger O'Keane) was born in County Derry, at the end of the 16th century. Heir to an entire barony, he was a very rich man and gifted on the harp.

When he first decided to move to Scotland he took with him a retinue and travelled in style. Happening to call one day, unattended, at the house of a certain Lady Eglinton, she, not knowing his rank, demanded a tune on the harp. Rory was offended and promptly left the house. When later the lady learned of his status, she made a formal apology and he, to show there were no hard feelings, made her this tune which he called in Latin "Da Mihi Manum" (Give Me Your Hand).

Rory won the favour of King James the VI during a visit to England, but apart from that trip south he spent the remainder of his life in Scotland, passing many years with MacDonald of Dunvegan on the Isle of Skye. He composed various tunes for the nobility which he called *Ports;* about a dozen of his pieces survive.

Scotland seems to have possessed a considerable appeal for Irish harpers of that period, as many of them spent time there or went there to live. Rory Dall went so far as to adopt the Scots name Morrison.

An odd quirk of fate placed him in the hour of his death, in Ayrshire, back at the house of Lady Eglinton again, where he breathed his last in the year of grace, 1653.

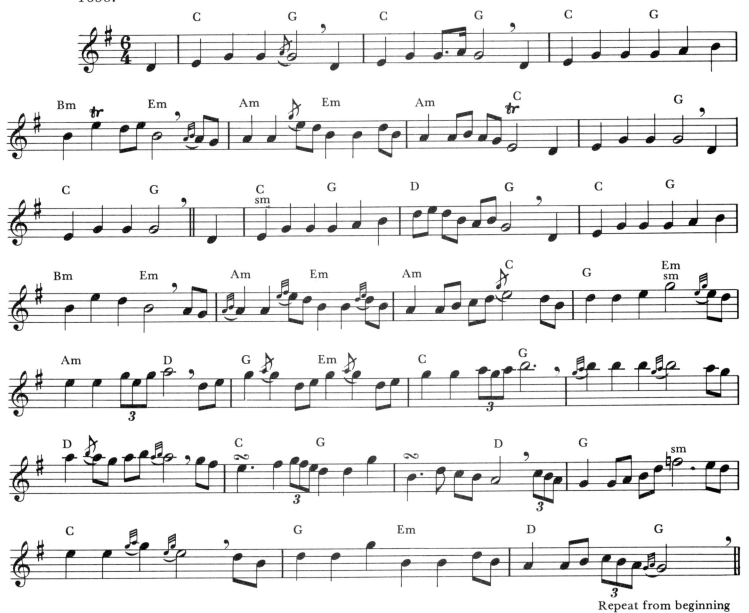

Repeat from beginning

THE DEW ON THE GRASS

This tune was noted by the Irish collector and flute player William Forde in the early 19th century. It has a similarity to a tune sometimes attributed to Carolan called "The Dark Plaintive Youth." This is an extremely lovely air, play it at a moderate speed.

FAREWELL

This final tune is a lovely old Gaelic air from the Scottish Highlands, usually known by its English title. The tune should go rather slowly.

Try playing it with practically no tonguing, providing articulation with cuts of L1 and L3 or double grace notes, etc., on most of the main notes. A pleasing tremolo effect can be gained on the long G's here by leaving an open hole below the G and trilling with R2. This is a nice effect that can be varied to suit other notes on other tunes.

In Conclusion

I suggest you listen to as many traditional players and recordings as possible, noting the way different instruments play the ornaments, particularly bagpipes. Copy hard till you develop your own certainty of how a tune should go.

One of the greatest of all 20th century whistle players was the Irish piper Willie Clancy. Listen to any records of his that you can get hold of. Recent recordings of Paddy Moloney, Sean Potts, and Michael Tubridy of the *Chieftains* and Cathal McConnell of *The Boys of the Lough* will prove very rewarding.

In playing with other instruments, if you find your whistle tends to be a little sharp of concert pitch you can flatten it by twisting the mouthpiece off a little. The mouthpiece is fixed on tight, so if it does not move easily loosen it by pouring a little cooking oil inside the whistle, leaving it there for a day or so; or dip the mouthpiece in hot *but not boiling* water.

If the mouthpiece gets really clogged, clear it with a pipe cleaner; you can also wash it out with soap every few years, whether it needs it or not. Make sure you get all the soap out or you'll be forever blowing bubbles.

There is a wide selection of whistles of different pitch, made to play different scales. The fingering used on the D whistle can be used on any other penny whistle, but the notes produced will be different. That is to say that any tune in this book, learned on the D whistle, can be played with the same fingering on a whistle of different pitch, but the tune will come out in a different key.

An advantage of having learned to read music for the D whistle is that there are an enormous number of fiddle tunes available which are written in one or two sharps.

Above all, share whatever you find out musically; you can't become less by giving away tunes or ideas. Always play as well as you can but remember the old cliche: "There will be someone better and worse than you." Or me.

You can always write to me at P.O. Box 27522, Los Angeles, California, 90027 (send a stamped self-addressed envelope). I'll personally answer all letters. Good luck.

Robin Williamson

Other Books You'll Want to Have . . .

O'Neill's Music of Ireland
by Miles Krassen
Here are over 1,000 jigs, reels, hornpipes, long dances and marches in a newly printed and corrected collection of the dance music of Ireland. This new and revised edition contains an introduction to the history of Irish music and tips on playing with an authentic feeling, plus new settings from the playing of Michael Coleman and the Sligo Fiddle Masters.

The English Concertina
by Richard Carlin
A complete instruction guide for beginning through advanced English concertina. Twenty-seven tunes are included, plus sections on harmony, drones, counterpoint, buying a concertina, repair hints, a bibliography, discography, and much more.

Gregorian Chants For Recorder
Edited and arranged by Stuart Isacoff
Throughout history, composers have employed Gregorian chants in their works. In this authentic volume, consistent with the actual rules of the times, Stuart Isacoff has arranged many important pieces for recorder, including the works of Guillaume de Machaut, Guillaume Dufay, Josquin Des Pres, J.S. Bach, and a wide variety of others. Every song has here been transcribed and arranged for the recorder for the first time. To even further increase the repertoire for recorder players, authentic chants are arranged in modern settings. The chants have been edited and arranged for solo, duet or trio playing; for soprano, alto or tenor recorder. Illustrated with facsimiles of original pieces.